Ready About!

Ready About!

MIKE PEYTON

Fernhurst Books

First published 1993 by
Fernhurst Books, 33 Grand Parade
Brighton, East Sussex

ISBN 0 906754 95 X

Composition by CST, Eastbourne
Printed by Ebenezer Baylis, Worcester
Printed and bound in Great Britain

To the crews from Crewe, Frampton
and Sparkhill Sailing Clubs

Acknowledgements
These cartoons are published with the kind permission of
Yachts & Yachting, Practical Boat Owner and *Yachting Monthly*,
where they first appeared.

Contents

—1—
TERRA FIRMA

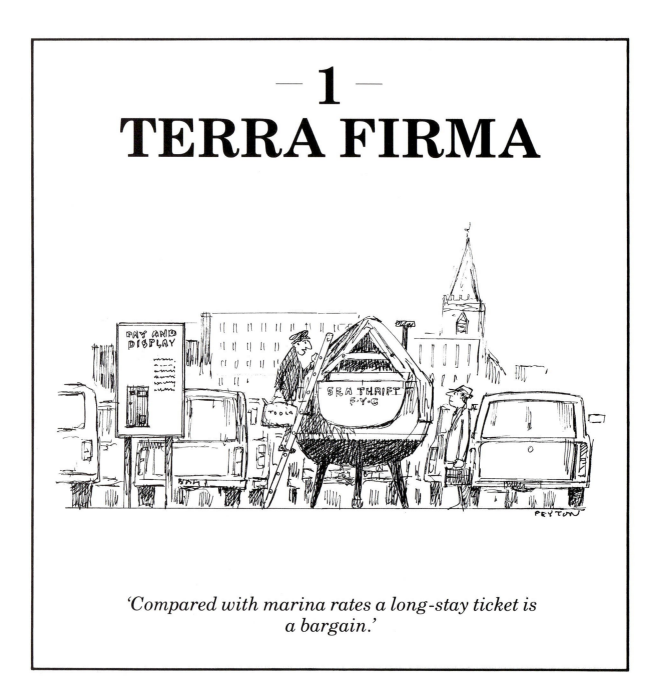

'Compared with marina rates a long-stay ticket is a bargain.'

'You're always the same when we're out of sight of
the boat . . . is she dragging? . . . no she isn't . . .
yes she is . . . no . . .'

'All we need is a Boat Jumble.'

'I'm sure he was a sailing man. He said, "That's enough, I only want a Sonata".'

'. . . A ten-metre sloop, fully comprehensive cover
– immediately . . .'

'It's a wonderful forecast: gales in all areas . . .'

'Shipping in a gale off The Nore.'

'I think that's Michael Fish he's hitting. He forecast sevens and eights this weekend, so George didn't sail.'

— 2 —
ALL CHOCKED UP

'I'm just moving this piece of wood, darling, so I can paint underneath.'

'The forecast said local showers.'

'It looks as if it will clear up for the drive home.'

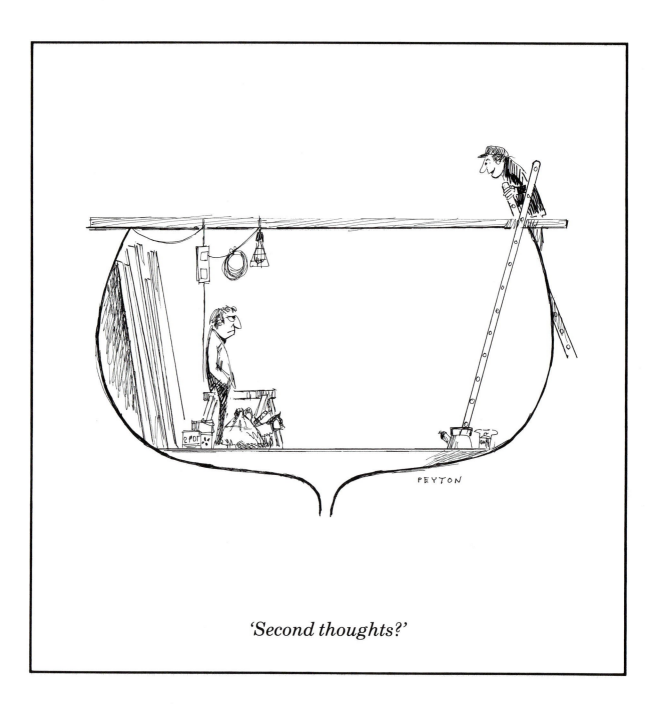

'Second thoughts?'

'Yet they do say he's a very good doctor . . .'

'It's a surprise. A Christmas party on board!'

'He must have rose-coloured binoculars . . .'

*'The only attraction about winter sailing is that
the parking's easier.'*

'Instead of worrying about what happened on the ebb, don't you think we should worry about what happens on the flood?'

— 3 —
THEY TIP OVER

'Looks like you got it wrong again.'

'You don't think they underestimate us?'

'I suppose it had to happen sometime for a
frostbite race . . .'

'This petty bureaucracy chokes me off . . .'

'We always relay the marks for open meetings.
That's where local knowledge comes in.'

*'It's the taking part that matters, not the winning
– right?'*

'I'd crew for you every weekend if the gravel pit
was like this.'

'Says he's a race officer – something about
a tally.'

'These charity races – children in need, etc. – are
marvellous excuses to get away from the kids . . .'

'So until the protest with the Lasers is sorted out
we'll go on to the 505s.'

— 4 —
IN DEEP WATER

'Have you ever wondered why it's so popular?'

'Of course I'm worried – a week of perfect weather, following winds, fair tides, spot-on navigation, not one single balls-up. I've cause to be worried.'

'Of course it's your bleeding fault, soon as you said "Good show, Froggy food for lunch".'

PEYTON

*'Cindy does all our navigation — you know what
kids are like with electronics.'*

'I wonder what he's being sick into?'

'Notice the next Service-by date – May '79?'

'I've had some absolute bargains from that
secondhand sail outfit.'

'John, I wonder if you'd mind coming into the cabin a minute. It's Janet, she's a bit sensitive.'

'Do you ever think there must be better ways of
spending fourteen grand?'

'It doesn't feel like a booming sport.'

'I thought we were in with a chance when you stopped praying and started composing a letter to your insurer . . .'

' *"If you need anything from below, just shout"* –
the smug b . . .'

'One must admit, going from waypoint to waypoint on autohelm takes the excitement out of sailing.'

'How about, as a joke, you tell them we've got rust holes?'

'Mark, Mark, quick – what shall I do?'

— 5 —
NIPS & TACKS

'How can you win in Burnham Week against those cheating b......s who don't drink and turn in early?'

'If they sailed like they drink, they'd be world beaters . . .'

'Where's that effing navigator?'

'All the others left it to starboard.'

*'It's in the bag, boys. Kite down, genny in,
gybe ove . . .'*

'I suppose it's some consolation that there are
others as stupid as us.'

'I see the training season is upon us: halves
instead of pints.'

'It's a pity you can't put the same effort into
trimming the garden as you put into trimming
your sails . . .'

'And I'm racing too so eff off!'

'Why doesn't the stubborn fool retire?'

'Now do you believe we're going the wrong way
round the island?'

— 6 —
STRIKE SOUNDINGS

'I'll be glad to get in. I've had enough excitement for one day.'

'Good trip?'

'Relax! I told you she'd stop ranging about when the tide turned.'

'I've brought our position up to date, John. Give
me a call when we sight land.'

'*They were a nice couple. I hope we meet them again sometime.*'

'How about waiting for the afternoon tide, Skip?'

'Steady with that courtesy flag, Joe.'

'Slow her down, Pete. Let's see how smart
Smartass is.'

'So much for your snug little anchorage.'

'Good, the fog's lifted.'

'It just says "Coastguard Aware".'

'What does it mean when the shipping forecast is
interrupted by Prayer for the Day?'

'To tell you the truth, I didn't think I would get
away with it.'

'I've seen all human life down there — passion, pride, aggression, jealousy, nationalism, romance . . .'

'Nice shot. Pity they're not closer.'

'Eight metres – and the dinghy?'

'That tip about tying a bucket to the stern of the tender has certainly quietened it down.'

' "If there's water for them, there's water for us",
that's what you said.'

— 7 —
MRS MATE

'On this tide? I'm doubtful, but I'll try.'

'This is the bit I like best.'

'Oh darling, we've just heard the forecast. Gales everywhere. We're so disappointed we won't be sailing..'

'I was just thinking, Brian. I sail to keep the
peace. Why do you do it?'

'Head to wind you said, and head to wind it is!'

'*Be interesting to see if she tips him in the dinghy or the drink.*'

'What did I tell you? It's made his Christmas – a
span of 3/8" calibrated galvanised chain.'

'It looks as if he has his bird down.'

'She says never mind excuses, the Maynards are
due at eight and you be there or else!'

'Just try and keep it from your father until after Christmas, otherwise we won't have a Christmas!'

'She says it's the recession. A new dress or a new
spinnaker – she got the old spinnaker.'

'We were thinking of having some person-
overboard drill, Joan.'

'Perhaps it is like a waterbed. But no.'